Benjamin Franklin

Thinker, Inventor, Leader

Jeanne Dustman

Consultant

Glenn Manns, M.A.
Teaching American History Coordinator
Ohio Valley Educational Cooperative

Publishing Credits

Dona Herweck Rice, *Editor-in-Chief*; Lee Aucoin, *Creative Director*; Conni Medina, M.A.Ed., *Editorial Director*; Jamey Acosta, *Associate Editor*; Neri Garcia, *Senior Designer*; Stephanie Reid, *Photo Researcher*; Rachelle Cracchiolo, M.A.Ed., *Publisher*

Image Credits

cover Library of Congress; p.1 Library of Congress; p.4 Library of Congress, LC-USZC4-7215; p.5 Joseph Sohm/Newscom; p.6 Wikimedia; p.7 Real Deal Photography/Shutterstock; p.8 Clipart.com; p.9 Library of Congress, LC-USZC4-7217; p.10 The Granger Collection; p.11 (top) PictureArts/Newscom, (bottom) Wongkaer/Dreamstime; p.12 The Granger Collection; p.13 The Granger Collection; p.14 Library of Congress, LC-USZ62-61782; p.15 ChipPix/Shutterstock; p.16 LawrenceLong/iStockphoto; p.17 (left) Imagebroker/Alamy, (right) Library of Congress, LC-DIG-hec-01525; p.18 Library of Congress, LC-USZ62-30750; p.19 Fesus Robert/Shutterstock; p.20 The Granger Collection; p.21 Amy Walters/Shutterstock; p.22 Shutterstock; p.23 (left) Library of Congress, LC-USZ62-45307, (right) Stephen Coburn/Shutterstock; p.24 Library of Congress, LC-USZ62-6078; p.25 Library of Congress, LC-DIG-pga-01591; p.26 Picture History/Newscom; p.27 (left) CNS Photo/Newscom, (right) Library of Congress, LC-USZC4-7214; p.28 (left) Library of Congress, LC-USZC4-7217, (right) Amy Walters/Shutterstock; p.29 (left) LawrenceLong/iStockphoto, (right) Shutterstock; p.32 Bainbridge Photo/London Ent/News

Teacher Created Materials
5301 Oceanus Drive
Huntington Beach, CA 92649-1030
http://www.tcmpub.com

ISBN 978-1-4333-1600-5

Printed by: 590835
Printed in: China

Table of Contents

Growing Up

Benjamin Franklin was born in 1706. He lived in Boston, Massachusetts (mas-uh-CHOO-sits). He had nine brothers and seven sisters.

Young Ben selling poems on the streets of Boston

Ben's home in Boston

Long ago, most boys went to work when they were young. Ben only went to school for one year. He liked to read and write.

Fun Fact

Children read from hornbooks. Hornbooks were wooden paddles with words on them.

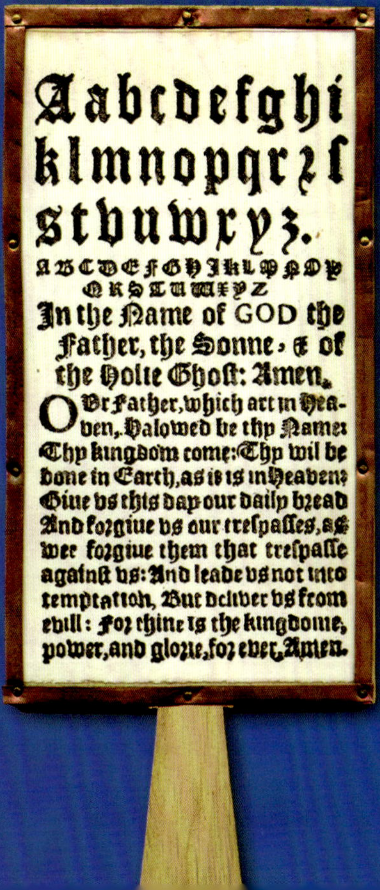

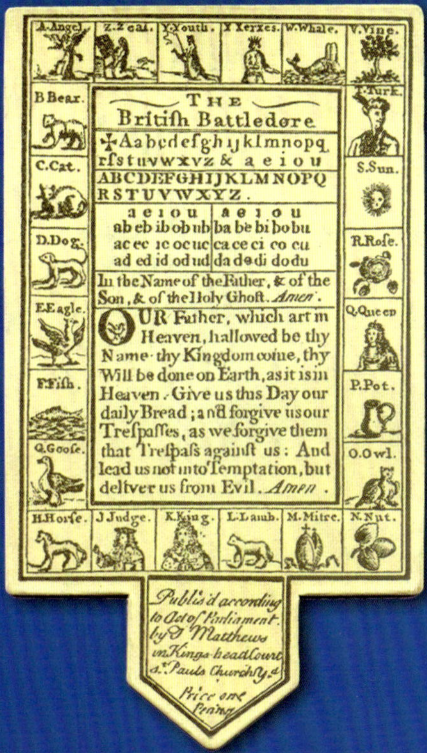

Fun Fact

Ben worked at his father's candle shop.

This picture shows how candles were made.

Ben did not like making candles. He went to work at his brother's print shop. One of his jobs was to print money. Soon Ben started his own print shop.

Ben outside his print shop

Ben the printer

New Ideas

Ben was an **inventor**. He had many good ideas. Ben worked hard to make his ideas come true. He started the first fire department in America. Ben started the first police force in Philadelphia (fill-uh-DEL-fee-uh), too.

An American fire engine from 1760

A police officer from the early 1900s

Fun Fact

Ben started the first street cleaning service, too.

Back then, books cost a lot of money. Most people did not own books. Ben and some friends opened a **library**. It was the first library in America. People could **borrow** books from the library.

Ben's library in Philadelphia

Ben inside the first library

Many Americans were poor. They needed help when they got sick. Ben and a friend started a **hospital**. At the hospital, doctors helped sick people get better.

Fun Fact

The hospital Ben started is still open today.

Ben's hospital

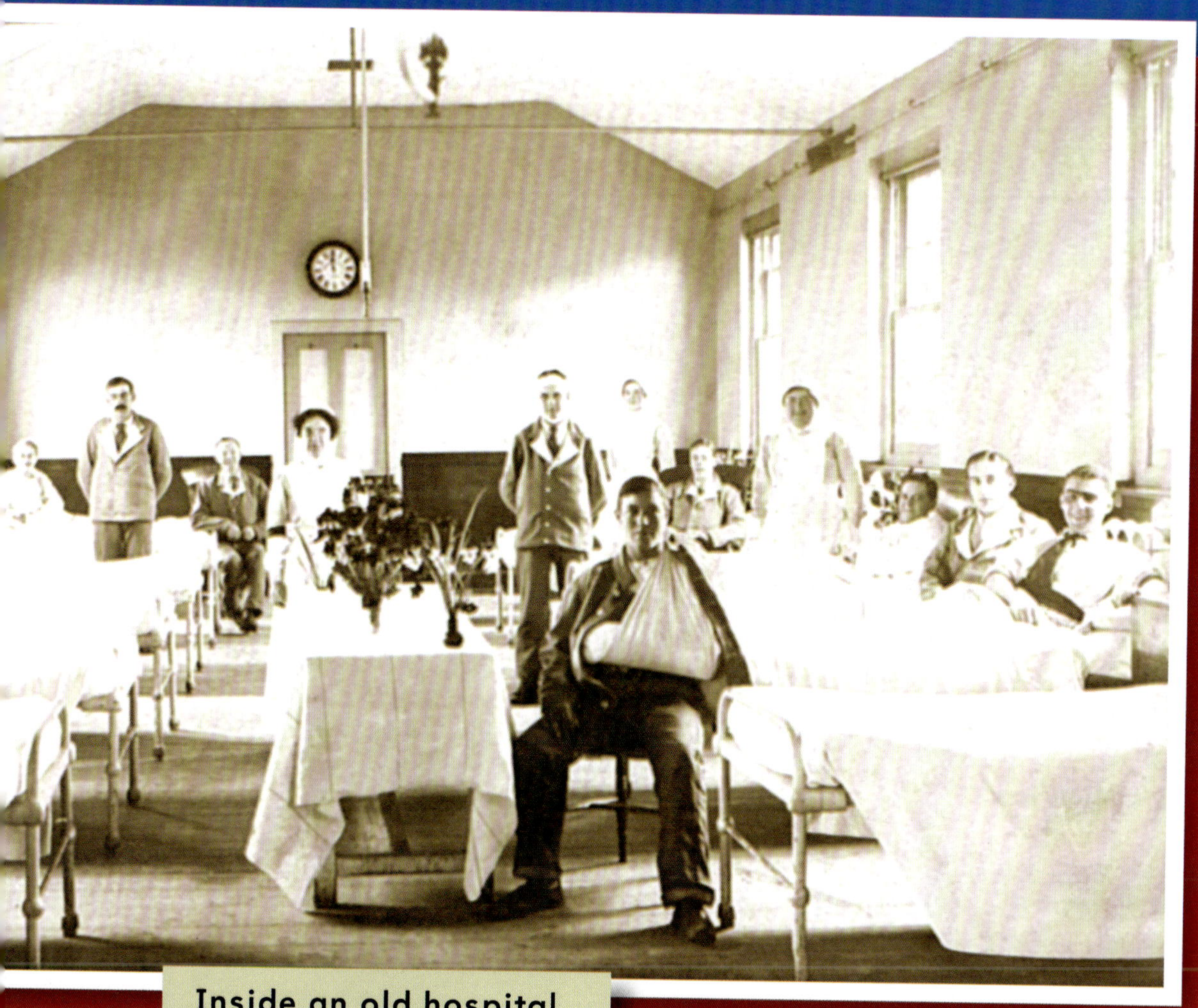

Inside an old hospital

Long ago, it was hard to send letters to people who lived far away. Ben started a new mail service. He was the first **postmaster** in Philadelphia.

A Benjamin Franklin postage stamp

A postwoman from 1916

A motorcycle postman from 1912

Inventor

Ben was **curious**. He put a key on a kite string. Lightning hit Ben's key. He got a shock. He found out that lightning is **electricity** (ee-lek-TRIS-ih-tee).

Ben and his son complete their experiment with a kite and key.

Lightning strikes!

Winters were cold. People needed heat. Ben the inventor made a new stove. It was cleaner than a fireplace. It made more heat, too.

A man using Ben's stove

A wood-burning stove

Leader

Ben helped write the **Declaration** (dek-luh-RAY-shuhn) **of Independence** (in-di-PEN-duhns). This letter said that America was free from Great Britain (BRIT-en). Great Britain did not want America to be free. A war started between the two countries.

IN CONGRESS, JULY 4, 1776.

The unanimous Declaration of the thirteen united States of America,

Declaration of Independence

Fun Fact

King George III of Great Britain ruled America.

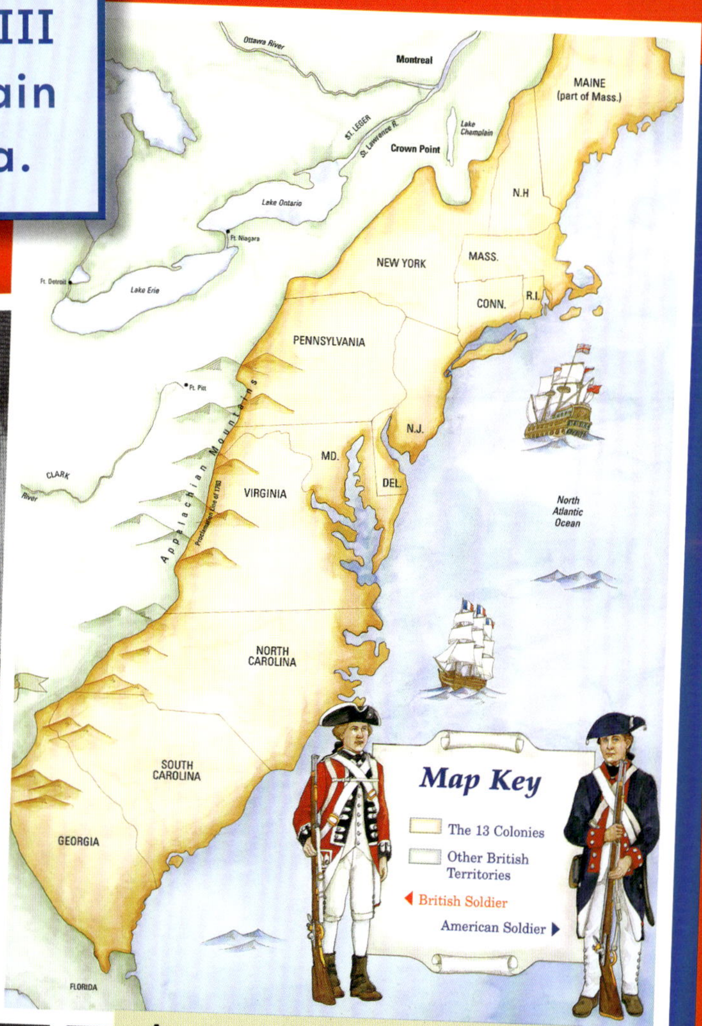

A map of the 13 colonies

King George III

America was losing the war. Ben met with the king of France. Ben asked the king to help America. France sent money and soldiers. They helped America beat Great Britain.

Ben at an important meeting

Ben at a party in France

America won the war. Ben was good at working with others. He worked with British leaders to write a peace **treaty**. The treaty said that America was free.

Fun Fact

The red marks below are wax. Long ago, people put wax next to their names on important papers. They put their fingerprint in the wax.

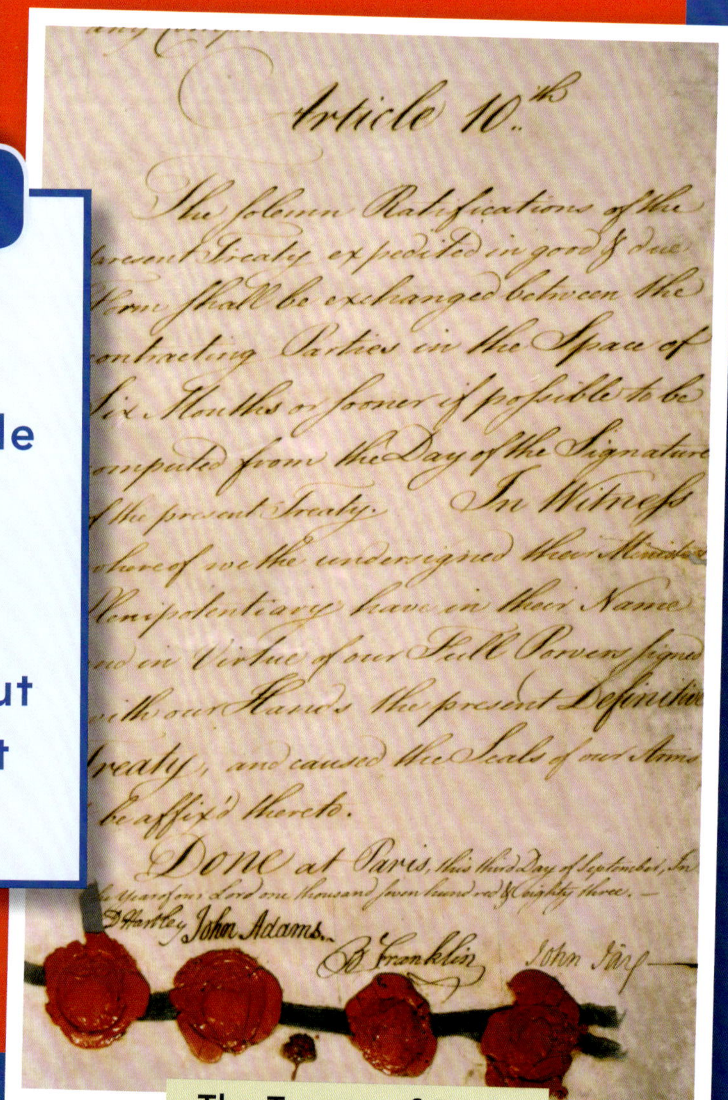

Article 10th.

The solemn Ratifications of the present Treaty expedited in good & due Form shall be exchanged between the contracting Parties in the Space of Six Months or sooner if possible to be computed from the Day of the Signature of the present Treaty. In Witness whereof we the undersigned their Ministers Plenipotentiary have in their Name and in Virtue of our Full Powers signed with our Hands the present Definitive Treaty, and caused the Seals of our Arms to be affix'd thereto.

Done at Paris, this third Day of September, In the Year of our Lord one thousand seven hundred & Eighty three.

D Hartley John Adams. B Franklin John Jay

The Treaty of Paris

Benjamin Franklin

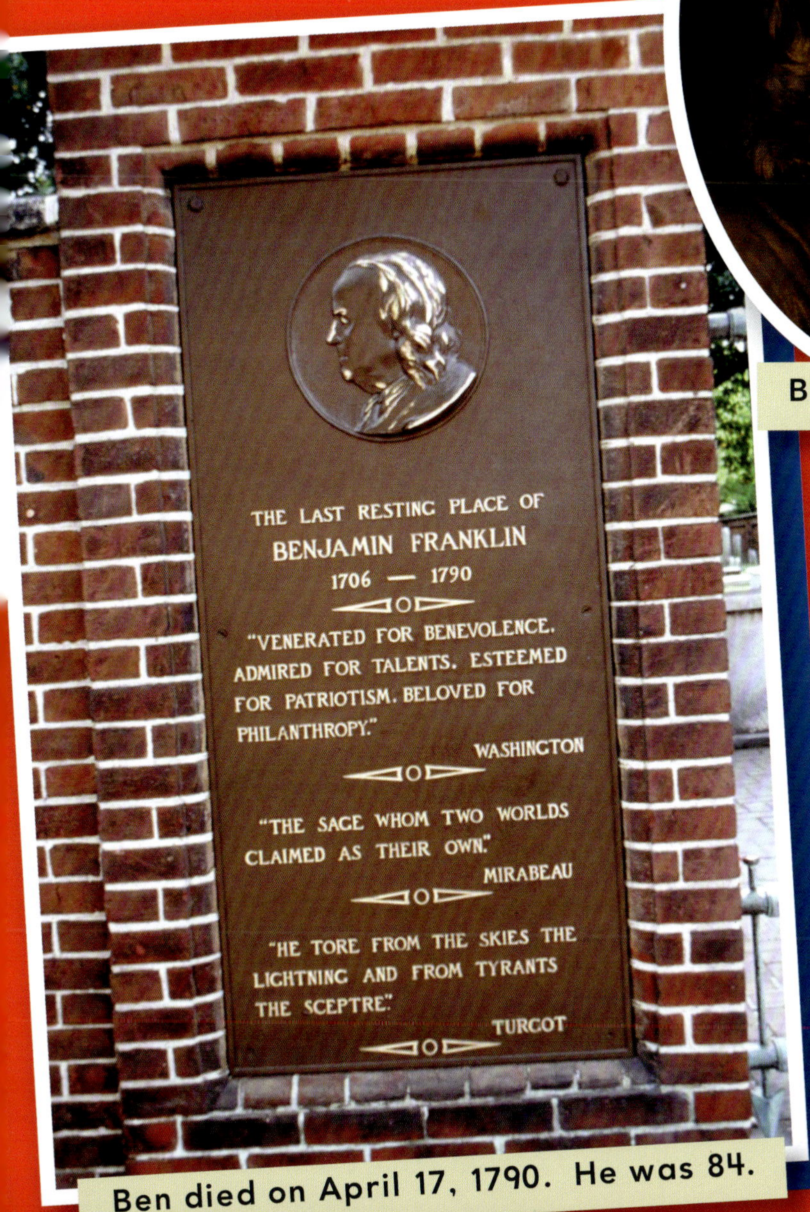

Ben died on April 17, 1790. He was 84.

Time

1706

Ben Franklin is born in Boston, Massachusetts.

1728

Ben starts his own print shop.

1737

Ben becomes the first postmaster in Philadelphia.

Line

IN CONGRESS, JULY 4, 1776.

The unanimous Declaration of the thirteen united States of Amer

1752

Ben becomes an inventor.

1776

Ben helps write the Declaration of Independence.

1790

Ben dies at the age of 84.

Glossary

borrow—to use something that belongs to someone else, such as a library book

Declaration of Independence—a paper people wrote to say that the 13 American colonies were free from Great Britain

electricity—a type of energy that travels through wires and makes things such as lights work

hospital—a place where sick or hurt people go to get better

inventor—a person who makes something new and different

library—a place that has books to read or borrow

postmaster—a person in charge of a post office

treaty—a formal agreement between two or more states or countries

Index

Americans Today

Dr. Patricia Bath is the first African American woman to create medical inventions. Her inventions have helped blind people see!